Salut Paris!

A Young Woman's Guide to Navigating French Life as an Expat in Paris

Savinee Srikham

First Editon 2024

Paris isn't just a city, it's a feeling, a test, and a thousand quiet discoveries waiting for you to notice. Here, the most ordinary days can turn extraordinary, and you'll find parts of yourself you didn't know were missing.

Content

Prologue

Are you ready to dive into a world of buttery *croissants*, *chic boutiques*, and cosy pavement *cafés*? Moving to a new country is a thrilling leap, but let's be honest—it's also a bit nerve-wracking, especially when that country is France. With its deep-rooted culture, love of fine wine, and streets brimming with history, Paris is like no other city. The allure of the City of Light is magical, but it takes a special kind of courage to call it home.

I was just twenty-one when I swapped the serene coastline of my small New Zealand town for the vibrant, bustling heart of Paris. I still remember that wild cocktail of emotions—equal parts excitement and *"What have I got myself into?"* Trading the laid-back rhythm of my hometown for the fast-paced heartbeat of a global city was a massive adjustment.

From the awe of seeing the *Eiffel* Tower sparkle against the night sky for the first time to the embarrassment of asking for a *préservatif* instead of jam at breakfast (so you're aware: *préservatif* means "condom" in French—cue the horror!), every day brought a new adventure, a fresh lesson, and plenty of moments that left me laughing or cringing at myself.

This book is a heartfelt guide drawn from my own journey as a young woman figuring out French life in Paris. From navigating the metro without looking like a complete tourist to breaking down language barriers, landing my first Parisian job, and finally discovering a place to call home, I'm here to share the ups, downs, and delicious in-betweens of making this city your own. My aim is to deliver practical tips and personal stories with a sprinkle of humour, so you can settle in a little more easily and embrace every quirky, charming corner of your new life in Paris. Let's make this adventure unforgettable—together.

And hey, it's completely normal to feel lost, homesick, or even a little daunted at times. These emotions are part of your ever-growing experience. Paris has a way of revealing the world—and yourself—in ways you never imagined. Along the way, you'll encounter moments of joy, frustration, and growth, and, like me, you might just find a little piece of yourself in the heart of this extraordinary city.

So, are you ready to make Paris your own?

Finding Your Temporary Home

Ah, Paris! The city of *baguettes*, quaint *bistros*, and streets bursting with timeless elegance and stunning architecture. If you're reading this, you're probably about to set foot in this magnificent city, armed with little more than a suitcase full of dreams—and perhaps a few too many pairs of shoes. In hindsight, I could have left behind three of the six pairs I'd crammed into my suitcase, but who knows when a Parisian fashion emergency might strike?

One of my first challenges in moving to Paris was finding somewhere to stay. While romantic notions of cosy rooftop apartments danced through my mind, the reality was far less glamorous—especially for a newcomer. Finding a temporary place to stay before my arrival quickly became my top priority.

Sitting in front of my laptop, endlessly scrolling through online listings, the reality of moving to a foreign city began to hit me. With each click, I felt I was teetering on the edge of either the adventure of a lifetime or a complete disaster. I was determined to find something that felt right—or at least looked good in the carefully curated photos. Eventually, I stumbled upon what seemed like the perfect spot: a single room in a shared family apartment on the outskirts of Paris, in *Levallois-Perret*, just a few kilometres

west of the city centre. It sounded ideal because, let's face it, affording even the tiniest studio in central Paris would have drained my savings faster than I could say "*bonjour*."

I sent off my standard set of questions to the host: Is there free Wi-Fi? Is the kitchen fully equipped? And, most importantly, how far is the nearest supermarket? (Priorities, right?) Once I got the all-clear, I eagerly clicked "book now," feeling as though I'd just secured my one-way ticket to the Parisian dream.

When I finally arrived at the Airbnb, I was greeted warmly by an older French gentleman whose limited English was just enough to put me at ease. As I climbed the flights of stairs (no lift, naturally —this is Paris, after all), I silently prayed the apartment would look as good as it had in the photos. To my relief, it was just right. Bright and (very!) colourful, and most importantly, clean.

My little room had a single bed, a desk, and best of all, a tall window overlooking a lively street and a charming café below. I could already picture myself sipping an espresso there in the mornings, pretending to read a French novel and effortlessly blending in with the locals—or so I hoped!

My advice? Don't stress too much about finding the 'perfect' place straight away. Start small, give yourself time to adjust to this incredible city, and dive into exploring all its quirks and charms. You can think about a more permanent place later.

For now, let's focus on helping you get your bearings and making the most of your first Parisian adventure.

Practical Tips
How to Secure Short-Term Rental in Paris

Here are some tried-and-tested websites to help you find a safe and comfortable place to stay before you arrive in Paris, along with tips to make the process easier:

- **Airbnb**: Best for flexible stays from a few days to several months—perfect for travellers or remote workers. **Tip:** Use the "monthly stays" filter if you're planning an extended stay. Look for Superhosts or properties with high ratings to ensure a hassle-free experience and prompt communication.

- **Booking.com**: Best for short stays, including hotels, apartments, and serviced flats. **Tip:** Look for fully furnished homes that provide more space and a kitchen if you're staying longer. Check reviews for insights about the property and the host.

- **Spotahome**: Best for medium-to-long-term rentals, ideal for stays of one month or more. **Tip:** They offer virtual tours and verified listings, so you can view the flat before committing. This is especially helpful for first-timers in Paris.

- **Paris Attitude**: Best for premium, fully furnished apartments for short and long-term stays. **Tip:** Great for professionals and expats, as they assist with essential paperwork like lease agreements—making your move smoother.

- **Lodgis**: Best for short-to-long-term furnished rentals. **Tip:** Lodgis provides multilingual support and helps with administrative processes, such as obtaining housing insurance. This is a valuable perk for newcomers.

Bonus Tip!

Consider broadening your search to neighbourhoods just outside the city centre, such as *Levallois-Perret, Courbevoie, Colombes, Montreuil, Montrouge,* or *Clichy*. These areas offer more affordable accommodation while still keeping you close to the heart of Paris. With Paris's efficient public transport system, you'll have no trouble commuting to the city centre. Plus, these areas often have a more relaxed vibe, giving you the best of both worlds.

Arriving in Paris, it's Your First Day

Before even stepping into my temporary Airbnb, my first day in Paris was already shaping up to be an unforgettable adventure. As I disembarked from the plane at Charles de Gaulle Airport, I felt a wave of emotions crash over me—excitement, nerves, and a fair bit of uncertainty. My Parisian chapter had officially begun, and I was equal parts thrilled and terrified.

The first victory of the day? Spotting my overstuffed suitcase on the conveyor belt. That burst of relief and joy? Absolutely real. With my luggage in tow, I headed towards the exit, bracing myself for the next challenge: figuring out how to get into the city. Taxis beckoned with their straightforward convenience, but I was determined to conquer the RER B train. After all, it was cheaper, faster, and felt like the proper Parisian way to start my adventure.

Standing before the ticket machine, I suddenly felt like a contestant on a game show. The challenge—Purchase a train ticket without making a complete fool of myself. The pressure of the queue behind me wasn't helping, and the screen, full of unfamiliar French phrases, might as well have been written in hieroglyphics.

After some frantic button-pushing and a silent prayer, I switched the machine to English, hoping for the best. Ticket in hand, I marched off to find the platform, feeling an odd mix of accomplishment and apprehension.

Once on the train, the scenery began to shift. The gritty outskirts of Paris, adorned with colourful graffiti, gave way to charming suburban houses, and then, finally, the iconic Parisian skyline began to peek through. My heart raced as we got closer. I was here—Paris, the City of Light! It was exhilarating, like the world had cracked open just for me.

Forty-five minutes later, I arrived at *Châtelet*, one of Paris's largest and busiest metro stations. The moment I stepped off the train, I was met with an overwhelming surge of people moving in every possible direction. It was chaos—but a thrilling kind. This was it, my baptism into the fast-paced Parisian life.

Châtelet isn't just a station; it's a labyrinth, an underground warren of endless corridors, countless exits, and signs pointing in every direction but the one you need. Locals darted around like they were late for a casting call in a Paris-themed action film, while wide-eyed tourists (like me) stumbled about, trying to make sense of it all. Google Maps had instructed me which metro line to take next, but the signage in *Châtelet* station? About as clear as instructions for assembling IKEA furniture in the dark.

With my suitcase trailing behind me, I clutched my belongings tightly, hyper-aware of every pickpocket horror story I'd ever read. My paranoia was matched only by my excitement as I scanned the station for clues. At one point, I realised I was on an escalator heading deeper underground when my line was actually a level above me. Perfect.

The summer heat didn't help matters. With no air conditioning in sight, the air felt thick and heavy, and I was convinced I'd entered some kind of metro sauna. My makeup? A distant memory. After what felt like a cardio workout disguised as a city welcome, I finally found the right platform. Triumph coursed through my veins as I collapsed onto a bench, sweating but victorious.

When the metro pulled up, its doors swished open, and I rushed inside like a triumphant gladiator stepping into the arena, grateful for even the slightest movement of air. I'd done it—against all odds, I was officially navigating Paris. Sort of.

Practical Tips
Getting from the Airport to Central Paris

If you find yourself wide-eyed, jet-lagged, and dragging an over-packed suitcase through Charles de Gaulle Airport, here are some tried-and-tested ways to reach the heart of Paris:

- **RER B Train** is one of the quickest and most budget-friendly ways to reach central Paris. Once you've heroically retrieved your luggage, follow the signs for the RER station in Terminal 2. At the ticket machine, be sure to switch it to English —unless deciphering French is part of your adventure—and grab your ticket. The train will zip you into the city in about 30–40 minutes. **Bonus tip:** Keep your ticket handy until you're completely out of the next station. Losing it could mean awkwardly holding up the exit gate while fumbling through your bags!

- **Roissybus**, If navigating a train feels like too much on Day One, the Roissybus is a solid alternative. It drops you off in the *Opéra* district, right in the heart of Paris. Buses run every 15–20 minutes, so you won't have to wait long. Just remember to buy your ticket at the airport before hopping aboard. The journey is smooth, and you can sit back and watch Paris start to unfold as you approach the city.

- **Airport Shuttle Services**, if you're travelling with a large group, want a more personalised experience, or are just simply too tired to be bothered by the city's public transportation, book a shuttle service in advance. Many companies offer shared or private rides that will take you directly to your accommodation.

- **Taxi Services**, if you've had enough adventure for one day—or if your suitcase looks like it could double as a piece of furniture—a taxi is your best bet. The flat fare from Charles de Gaulle to central Paris is typically between €50–€60. Follow the signs to the official taxi stand (ignore anyone offering you a *"special deal"*), and enjoy the luxury of door-to-door service. Treat yourself—you've earned it!

Understanding the City's Layout

Paris is a city like no other, with its twenty *arrondissements* (districts) spiralling out from the city centre in a clockwise fashion, much like the intricate hands of a vintage clock. Each district is its own little universe, offering a unique slice of Parisian life. Whether you're wandering through the historic charm of *le Marais* (3rd & 4th *arrondissements*) or soaking up the bohemian spirit of *Montmartre* (18th *arrondissement*), every corner of Paris has its own story to tell.

At the heart of it all flows the *Seine* River, Paris's shimmering ribbon of life, cutting the city into two distinct halves: the *Rive Gauche* (Left Bank) and the *Rive Droite* (Right Bank). The Left Bank oozes creativity and intellectual charm—this is where philosophers, writers, and artists once gathered to sip wine and argue passionately in the cosy cafés of *Saint-Germain-des-Prés*. Bookshops like Shakespeare and Company still carry that spirit, making it the perfect place to lose yourself (and your travel budget) in the smell of old pages and literary dreams.

The Right Bank, by contrast, is the epitome of Parisian glamour.

With its chic boutiques, bustling business hubs, and avenues like the iconic *Champs-Élysées*, it has a more polished, vibrant energy. And then there's *Montmartre*, where winding streets lead you to the stunning *Sacré-Cœur Basilica* and artists set up easels to capture Paris's ethereal beauty.

Think of the Left Bank and Right Bank as your treasure maps to the city's iconic landmarks. Want to marvel at the *Eiffel* Tower, explore the literary past of the Latin Quarter, or bask in the gothic glory of *Notre-Dame* Cathedral? The Left Bank has your back. Prefer to lose yourself in the grandeur of the *Louvre*, shop until you drop along *Rue Saint-Honoré*, or climb the hilly magic of *Montmartre*? You'll find all that and more on the Right Bank.

Once you understand Paris's layout, you'll feel like a seasoned local, confidently hopping from one *arrondissement* to another without breaking a sweat—or at least not before your second *pain au chocolat* of the day. Save your energy for wandering cobblestone streets, people-watching at bustling cafés, and diving into the vibrant markets (trust me, they'll call your name).

Most Parisian streets have signs with *arrondissement* numbers, so you'll always know where you are in the city's spiral. For instance, if you're in the 5th *arrondissement*, you're right in the heart of the Latin Quarter, surrounded by history and academia. If you're in the 16th, welcome to a residential area full of understated elegance.

Paris is a patchwork of moments waiting to be discovered. Each *arrondissement* has its own rhythm, personality, and secrets, so don't be afraid to get a little lost—sometimes, that's when the magic really begins.

Practical Tips
A Brief Overview of the 20 Arrondissements

To give you a head start on your Parisian adventures, here's a brief overview of the twenty arrondissements, along with some personal tips to help you unlock the magic of this enchanting city:

1er Arrondissement (Louvre): Home to the iconic *Louvre* Museum, this central district is a hub of art, history, and culture. You can explore the beautiful *Tuileries* Garden, enjoy fine dining, and stroll along the *Seine*. Be sure to take a moment to admire the gleaming glass pyramid. For a unique experience, consider visiting the nearby *Palais Royal*, where you can wander through its elegant gardens and enjoy the striking *Colonnes de Buren* installation.

2ème Arrondissement (Bourse): Known for its historic stock exchange and stunning architecture, it features the vibrant shopping district of *Les Halles* and the trendy *Rue Montorgueil*. It's lined with traditional French food shops, including *boulangeries* (bakeries), *fromageries* (cheese stores), and *pâtisseries* (pastry shops). Don't forget to explore the picturesque *Place des Victoires*, a charming square surrounded by elegant buildings, which adds to the district's allure. If you're on a pastry pilgrimage, this is the perfect place to start!

3ème Arrondissement (Le Marais): A chic neighbourhood brimming with stylish boutiques, art galleries, and charming cafés. It's also home to the *Picasso* Museum and the historic *Place des Vosges*. Don't miss the vibrant *Marché des Enfants Rouges*, where you can sample delicious local delicacies. This area is perfect for strolls, enjoying a coffee, and immersing yourself in the artistic vibe, beret optional!

4ème Arrondissement (Ile de la Cité and Ile Saint-Louis): This *arrondissement* includes the beautiful *Ile de la Cité*, home to *Notre-Dame* Cathedral, and the whimsical *Ile Saint-Louis*, known for its charming streets and ice cream shops. Make sure to indulge in a scoop (or two!) of the famous *Berthillon* ice cream, it's a rite of passage!

5ème Arrondissement (Latin Quarter): Famous for its vibrant student life and bustling nightlife, the Latin Quarter is home to *Sorbonne* University, the *Panthéon*, and countless beloved bookshops. The area's charming, narrow streets invite exploration, with cosy cafés and vintage shops at every turn. For a dose of history, check out the ancient Roman Baths at the *Musée de Cluny*, adding a touch of antiquity to this lively neighbourhood.

6ème Arrondissement (Saint-Germain-des-Prés): A historic hub for intellectuals and artists, this area is known for its iconic literary cafés, chic art galleries, and trendy boutiques. Don't miss the stunning *Luxembourg* Gardens and the historic Church of *Saint-Germain-des-Prés*, one of the oldest churches in Paris. For a true taste of Parisian culture, stop by *Café de Flore* or *Les Deux Magots*, where famous writers and philosophers once gathered.

7ème Arrondissement (Eiffel Tower): Home to the iconic *Eiffel* Tower, this district is known for its elegant avenues, cultural landmarks, and renowned museums like the *Musée d'Orsay* and the stunning *Hôtel des Invalides*, where Napoleon is buried. If you're feeling brave, try to tackle the stairs of the *Eiffel* Tower for a rewarding view. Afterwards, take a stroll along the *Champs de Mars* gardens, perfect for a picnic with a view of the tower and a prime spot to watch it light up in the evening.

8ème Arrondissement (Champs-Élysées): Famous for the iconic *Champs-Élysées* and the majestic *Arc de Triomphe*, this upscale district is celebrated for its luxury shopping, elegant theatres, and a vibrant nightlife scene. Whether you're browsing designer stores or enjoying a night out, this area is sure to dazzle. After indulging in retail therapy, consider catching a show at the historic *Palais des Congrès* or savouring a fine dining experience at one of the chic restaurants lining the avenue, where you can enjoy delicious French cuisine with a view of the bustling street life.

9ème Arrondissement (Opéra): The area houses the *Palais Garnier*, an iconic opera house known for its opulent design. It's a vibrant district filled with shopping and entertainment options, including the *Galeries Lafayette*, where you can find luxury brands beneath a stunning glass dome. Don't miss the enchanting Christmas decorations that adorn the streets during the winter holiday season and admire the breathtaking architecture that defines this elegant part of Paris!

10ème Arrondissement (Canal Saint-Martin): The *Canal Saint-Martin* runs through this trendy area, known for its hip cafés, boutiques, and relaxed atmosphere. This area is a popular spot for picnics and walks along the water, making it perfect for unwinding. Grab a sandwich and enjoy a sunny afternoon by the canal, where you can watch boats glide by and soak in the charming vibe of the neighbourhood!

11ème Arrondissement (Bastille): Famous for its vibrant nightlife and diverse dining options, the area around *Place de la Bastille* is bustling with activity after dark. You'll find a variety of restaurants serving everything from traditional French cuisine to international dishes. It's also home to the historic *Bastille* Opera,

where you can watch world-class performances. If you're in the mood for an unforgettable night out, this is the spot for dancing and cosy wine bars.

12ème Arrondissement (Bercy): Known for its expansive *Parc de Bercy*, where you can enjoy beautiful gardens, scenic walking paths, and the *Bercy Village* shopping area. It's also home to the AccorHotels Arena, which hosts a variety of concerts and events throughout the year. This vibrant area is perfect for a day of exploring, dining, and entertainment.

13ème Arrondissement (Butte-aux-Cailles): Renowned for its vibrant Chinatown, home to one of the largest Asian communities in the city, offering a variety of Asian restaurants and markets. It boasts an impressive street art scene, particularly in the *Butte-aux-Cailles* area, where large murals add colour to the neighbourhood. The *Bibliothèque François Mitterrand,* a modern architectural landmark, houses one of France's largest libraries. Be sure to take your camera, you'll want to capture all the vibrant street art!

14tème Arrondissement (Montparnasse): Historically, an artistic neighbourhood, *Montparnasse* is home to the towering *Tour Montparnasse* and the famous *Cimetière du Montparnasse*, where many artists are buried. The area also features the lovely *Parc Montsouris*, a serene space ideal for strolls and picnics, offering magnificent views of the city. If you're up for it, climb to the top of the Tour for a breathtaking panorama!

15ème Arrondissement (Vaugirard): A primarily residential area, the 15th features the *Parc André Citroën*, one of Paris's most modern parks, complete with expansive lawns, themed gardens,

and the *Ballon de Paris*, a tethered hot air balloon that offers panoramic views of the city. This park is a lovely escape from the hustle and bustle, providing a serene environment for picnics and strolls. Nearby, you can also explore the charming streets of the neighbourhood, dotted with local bakeries and cafés, where you can savour fresh pastries and watch the world go by.

16ème Arrondissement (Passy): Famous for its upscale residential neighbourhoods and elegant architecture, featuring wide boulevards and beautiful Haussmannian buildings. It is home to several iconic landmarks, including the *Palais de Tokyo*, the *Musée Marmottan Monet*, and the stunning *Trocadéro* Gardens, which offer breathtaking views of the *Eiffel* Tower. The 16th is also known for its lush parks, such as *Parc de Bagatelle* and *Bois de Boulogne*, making it a popular area for walks and picnics.

17ème Arrondissement (Batignolles): Known for its charming neighbourhoods like *Batignolles* and *Parc Monceau*, blending residential tranquillity with vibrant local life. It features the grand *Palais des Congrès*, a major venue for conferences, and the historic *Rue de Levis*, renowned for its bustling market atmosphere. Be sure to visit *Parc Monceau*, a beautiful park ideal for strolls and picnics among stunning statues.

18ème Arrondissement (Montmartre): Famous for the stunning *Sacré-Cœur Basilica* and its rich artistic history, *Montmartre* is a charming district filled with narrow streets and a vibrant nightlife scene. As you wander the cobblestone paths, keep an eye out for the many street artists showcasing their talents at *Place du Tertre*, where you can even commission a quick portrait!

19ème Arrondissement (La Villette): A cultural hub, home to the expansive *Parc de la Villette*, which offers a variety of cultural

events and outdoor activities, making it ideal for families and nature lovers. The area features the *Cité des Sciences et de l'Industrie*, one of Europe's largest science museums with interactive exhibits, and the *Philharmonie de Paris*, a beautiful concert hall that hosts diverse shows. It's a lively area for exploration and family-friendly fun.

20ème Arrondissement (Ménilmontant): This is a lively and artistic district known for its vibrant atmosphere and diverse community. The area is home to *Père Lachaise* Cemetery, where famous figures like Oscar Wilde and Jim Morrison are buried. It's a peaceful spot to wander. The streets are filled with quirky cafés, independent art galleries, and a youthful energy that makes it a great place to explore. When night falls, *Ménilmontant* comes alive with a variety of bars, live music venues, and restaurants serving international dishes and French classics. Whether you're enjoying a casual drink with friends or grabbing a bite to eat, the district's laid-back vibe makes it an ideal spot for a fun night out.

Bonus Tips!

Paris is a maze of charming, winding streets that can easily leave you feeling lost—both figuratively and literally. While wandering aimlessly might just lead you to a hidden gem of a café or the perfect gelato stand, it's always better to have a bit of direction when exploring, especially if you're aiming to see specific sights. Trust me, a little pre-planning can make your Paris experience much more enjoyable and efficient. And don't worry, if you do end up lost, you'll probably find something wonderful along the way. But if you'd like to avoid that mystical lost-in-Paris feeling, here are two apps to help guide you to your next adventure:

- **Citymapper** is your ultimate travel companion for navigating Paris's public transport network. Whether hopping on a bus, catching the metro, or even taking a train, this app provides real-time updates, alternate routes, and estimated travel times. It's like having a Parisian guide in your pocket. Plus, it even suggests the best modes of transport based on the traffic situation, so you can save time and avoid getting stuck in the metro.

- **Bonjour RATP**, if you're planning to ride the metro, this is the app you want to have. It's specifically designed to help you navigate the entire metro system. With real-time updates, route planning, and even the option to buy your metro tickets in advance, Bonjour RATP is a must-have. No more scrambling for coins at the ticket machine—simply scan your QR code when you enter the station, and you're ready to go!

So, before you step out the door, make sure you've got your navigation apps ready. With a little prep and a handy map (or your phone), you'll be breezing through Paris in no time. But always remember—Paris is a city to be savoured, so while efficiency is key, don't rush through it. Stop for a café, take in the sights, and embrace the adventure!

Navigating the City Like a Local

Mastering Paris's public transport felt like earning my unofficial badge as a local. The first time I navigated the city solo, I felt terrified and accomplished, like I had cracked a code that Parisians understood!

Initially, exploring the city alone was daunting. Every corner seemed to hide a new challenge, and crossing the *Seine* multiple times in one day made me feel like I was constantly circling back to square one. But as I continued my wandering, a sense of freedom began to wash over me. Each successful excursion lifted my spirits and deepened my sense of belonging in this vibrant city. It wasn't just the sights that kept me going; it was the tiny victories —like nervously ordering my breakfast in broken French or taking the metro in the right direction—that reminded me that I was learn-ing, growing, and truly finding my place.

As I gained confidence in using the city's public transport, I picked up a few essential tips that made life much easier. The *Paris Métro* is iconic, and once you get the hang of it, it's your best friend. It may look like a rainbow spiderweb at first, but trust me, it's more intuitive than it seems.

The secret? Always check the line's final station to make sure you're headed in the right direction. It's better than accidentally touring the suburbs-unknown when you meant to visit *le Louvre*!

Another helpful quirk: metro doors don't always open automatically. Be ready to push a button or pull a lever when the train stops—think of it as a little puzzle to solve. And while the metro is safe and efficient, I recommend avoiding rush hours when it's packed and pickpockets are at their busiest, especially at popular stations like *Gare du Nord* and *Châtelet*. If you must travel during peak times, keep your bag close and in sight!

Practical Tips
Navigating Paris Like a Pro

Navigating Paris isn't as intimidating as it seems. With some preparation and a sense of adventure, you'll soon be breezing through the city like a local. Here's how to make public transport your best friend:

- **Purchase a Navigo Pass:** This is a game-changer for unlimited travel on the city's public transport. Available for a week or a month, it's cost-effective, especially if you plan to explore extensively.

- **Go Digital with Mobile Payment Options:** Skip the hassle of paper tickets by loading your Navigo Pass or metro tickets onto your phone through the RATP app or Bonjour RATP app. It's easy and stress-free—no more scrambling for paper tickets!

- **Leverage Google Maps:** It's your ultimate companion for Parisian public transport. Google Maps offers real-time updates on arrivals, best transport options, and step-by-step walking directions. **Pro tip:** download offline maps before you go, so you're covered even without mobile data.

- **Time Your Journeys Wisely:** Public transport gets packed during rush hours (weekdays from 7:30 to 9:30 am and 5:00 to 7:00 pm). Plan your trips outside these windows to avoid the crowds and enjoy a more comfortable ride.

Bonus Tips!
Fun and Eco-Friendly Ways to Explore

If you're looking for something a bit more adventurous, exploring Paris on electric bikes or scooters is a fast and eco-friendly way to see the city. It's a unique perspective and a great alternative to crowded public transport. Here are some fantastic options:

- **Vélib' Métropole:** Rent city bikes through the Vélib' app, which shows nearby bike stations and available options. If you want a boost, the green electric bikes are perfect for tackling hilly streets!

- **Jump by Uber:** Jump offers electric bikes with a user-friendly app. You can easily find, unlock, and ride these bikes, enjoying the added power of an electric motor—perfect for longer rides or casual exploration.

- **Dott:** Specialising in electric bikes, and can provide a seamless experience for city commuting. The app lets you quickly locate and rent bikes, making it easy to zip around Paris.

- **Lime:** For those who prefer scooters, this is the go-to choice. Rent electric scooters for short distances or to skip crowded metro rides. Plus, they're eco-friendly—good for both you and the planet!

Whether you're gliding through the streets on a bike or scooter, these options let you explore Paris at your own pace while enjoying a fun and sustainable way to travel. Happy riding!

Bonus Tip for Scenic Travel!

For a more scenic route, opt for the bus. They're slower but offer the perfect opportunity to enjoy Paris as you travel. When you're at the stop, don't forget to raise your hand to signal the driver, greet them with a friendly *"bonjour,"* and press the red button to signal your stop. Also, always validate your ticket or metro pass before hopping on—random checks happen, and the fines for non-compliance are hefty!

Shopping for Groceries in Paris

Grocery shopping in Paris is more than just ticking off items on a list—it's a mini adventure that lets you dive head-first into the city's rich culinary world. Whether you're a seasoned chef or just mastering the art of picking up a *baguette* without feeling too awkward, shopping for food in Paris is an experience you'll come to cherish. Of course, there are your everyday supermarkets, but nothing beats the charm of Paris's open-air markets. Picture this: vibrant fruit stalls, the irresistible scent of fresh herbs, bread and cheeses that are more art than food, and pastries so delicate that you'll have a hard time not taking a photo before you take your first bite.

Here, grocery shopping is almost a social ritual. Don't be shy—greet the vendors with a hearty "*bonjour*!" and, if you're feeling extra Parisian, tuck your reusable bag neatly under your arm. You'll blend in like a local, and maybe even get a few tips from the vendor on how to best prepare those delicious tomatoes or pair the perfect wine with your cheese. Yes, it's true—shopping for groceries in Paris is as much about connecting with the community as it is about filling your fridge.

Practical Tips
Grocery Store Options

In Paris, picking up groceries is more than a chore, it's a cultural experience. And if you're planning to pick up a *baguette* or two, remember to hold it proudly under your arm! Here are some practical tips and advice to help you manage grocery shopping in Paris, along with options for several types of shops available in the city:

- **Supermarkets (*Supermarchés*), Carrefour, Monoprix** and **Franprix,** are the most common supermarket chains, offering a wide range of products from fresh produce to pantry staples. Monoprix is often seen as slightly more upscale, with a broad selection of organic and international foods, while Franprix tends to be more convenient for quick stops in smaller neighbourhoods. **Tip:** Supermarkets usually close by 9 or 10 pm and are often closed on Sundays or have reduced hours. Be sure to plan to avoid last-minute shopping struggles.

- **Local Markets (*Marchés*),** Paris is home to numerous open-air markets where you can buy fresh fruit, vegetables, meats, cheeses, and other speciality items directly from vendors. **Tip:** Markets are typically open from early morning until around 1 or 2 pm, and many are closed on Mondays. It's best to arrive early to get the freshest produce. Some well-known markets include: *Marché d'Aligre* (12th *Arrondissement*) is affordable and diverse, *Marché Bastille* (11th *Arrondissement*) is one of the city's largest and most popular markets, *Marché Rue Mouffetard* (5th *Arrondissement*) is known for its traditional French produce.

- **Discount Supermarkets,** such as **Lidl** and **Aldi**, are great options if you're on a budget. They offer a wide selection of affordable groceries, including fresh produce, dairy, and basic household items. **Tip:** While these supermarkets are cheaper, they might not have as wide a selection of speciality items compared to bigger chains like Carrefour or Monoprix.

- **Organic Stores (*Magasins Bio*),** like ***Naturalia*** and ***Bio c' Bon.*** Organic food is quite popular in Paris, and these chains specialise in organic and eco-friendly products. You'll find fresh produce, organic dairy, healthy foods, and eco-conscious household products. **Tip:** While organic shops are more expensive, they are great for those looking for organic, gluten-free, or vegan options

Specialty Shops

Speciality shops across the city offer unparalleled quality, authentic flavours, and a true taste of French culture. Whether you're after artisanal cheeses, freshly baked bread, or expertly selected wines, these shops are where locals go to find the best. Here's a guide to help you navigate some of Paris' finest speciality stores:

- *Fromageries* (**Cheese Shops**), Paris is heaven for cheese lovers. Head to shops like *Laurent Dubois* or *Barthélemy* to find an incredible variety of French cheeses.

- *Boulangeries* (**Bakeries**), every neighbourhood have their local bakeries where you can get fresh bread and pastries.

- *Boucheries* (**Butchers**), local butcher shops often offer a wider variety and higher-quality cuts than supermarkets. Ask for recommendations to discover excellent beef, lamb, or poultry.

- *Cavistes* (**Wine Shops**), while supermarkets sell wine, for more personalised advice, or special bottles, head to a local wine shop like *Nicholas* or smaller independent stores for expert guidance.

- *Poissonneries* (**Fish Markets**), for seafood, visit a *poissonnerie*. Try *Poissonnerie de l'Opéra* in the 2nd, or *La Poissonnerie du Marché* in the 11th for a variety of fish and shellfish.

- *Picard*, specialising in high-quality frozen foods. Offers a wide selection of frozen meals, vegetables, and desserts. It's a convenient option for quick meals that you can heat up at home or work.

Ethnic and International Grocery Stores

Paris is a melting pot of cultures, and its diverse grocery stores reflect this beautifully. Whether you're craving authentic Asian spices, Italian delicacies, or Middle Eastern treats, the city offers an array of shops that bring global flavours to your doorstep. Here are some of the best places to find international ingredients and discover a world of culinary inspiration:

- **Tang *Frères* (13th *Arrondissement*),** one of the largest Asian supermarkets in Paris, specialising in Chinese and Southeast Asian products.

- ***La Grande Épicerie* (7th *Arrondissement*),** is a gourmet supermarket with a fantastic selection of international foods, perfect for finding hard-to-source ingredients or splurging on gourmet treats.

- **Eataly (4th *Arrondissement*),** is an Italian food haven offering everything from fresh pasta, Italian wines, and cheeses to pantry staples imported from Italy. Great for authentic Italian ingredients and a selection of ready-to-eat items.

- ***Épiceries/Suprette* (In your neighbourhood),** these small stores are great for late-night shopping and tend to have a mix of essentials, fresh produce, and Middle Eastern ingredients.

- **Korean Supermarket (Throughout Paris),** for a variety of Korean ingredients, head to one of my favourites, **K-Mart,** in the 1st *Arrondissement*. This supermarket offers a wide range of Korean snacks, sauces, fresh produce, and prepared meals ready to enjoy.

- **Izrael (4th *Arrondissement*)** is known as *L'épicerie du Monde,* this charming shop specialises in Middle Eastern, Mediterranean, and North African products. From spices and olives to dried fruits and speciality sauces, Izrael is a treasure trove for discovering flavours from around the globe, all in a cosy, old-world setting.

Bonus Tips!

- **Reusable Bags,** France has strict regulations on plastic bags, so bring your own reusable bags for groceries. If you forget, you'll often need to purchase a reusable bag in-store. Tote bags or foldable bags are great to always carry with you, as you might find yourself spontaneously grocery shopping.

- **Loyalty Cards,** many supermarkets offer loyalty cards that provide discounts and promotions. Signing up can be worth it, especially if you shop at the same place frequently.

- **Price Awareness,** prices can vary widely between supermarkets and local markets. Shopping at open-air markets or discount supermarkets like Lidl will give you better deals on fresh produce than upscale stores. Compare prices for staples like milk, eggs, and vegetables across different shops to find the best bargains.

- **Consider Online Grocery Delivery,** services like **Carrefour Drive, Monoprix.fr,** and **Amazon** Fresh allow you to order groceries online and have them delivered to your door. This is convenient for heavy or bulk items and especially helpful if you're busy or prefer to avoid carrying groceries on public transportation.

Always greet shopkeepers with a *"bonjour"* when you enter a store, it's non-negotiable in Paris and sets the tone for friendly service. Be aware that many smaller shops and cafés still prefer cash, so always keep a few Euros in your wallet.

Familiarise yourself with store hours, as Parisian shops and restaurants often have irregular closing times. Checking in advance will save you the frustration of arriving at a closed door when you need groceries or a late meal.

Don't forget about your neighbourhood *boulangerie* for daily bread (because yes, it's normal to buy a fresh *baguette* every single day here) and local *fromageries* for an endless selection of delicious cheeses. And if you ever need something at odd hours, look for an *épicerie* or *superette*, those small convenience stores dotted around the city can be lifesavers.

Manoeuvring the Streets
During a Protest

What I thought would be a quiet, relaxing morning, a simple stroll near the *Arc de Triomphe*, quickly transformed into an unexpected, heart-pounding adventure. Coming out of the metro to find the streets filled with energy I hadn't anticipated, and before I knew it, I was in the middle of a full-blown protest. As the early morning calm dissolved into shouts, whistles, and the unmistakable sting of tear gas in the air, I found myself ducking behind a corner as a mini-civil war exploded close by. This was not the Paris I had seen on postcards! Welcome to Paris where protests are as common as *croissants*.

Protests are a deeply ingrained part of French culture, a way for people to voice their opinions on everything from labour strikes to environmental movements. While some protests are peaceful, others feel like you've walked into a chaotic movie set. One minute, you're sipping your coffee, and the next, you're running for cover. Lesson learned, always check the news before leaving the house!

Despite the occasional chaos, there's something undeniably inspiring about the spirit of protest here. Yes, it can be intense, but it's also a testament to the French commitment to fighting for justice and change. It's a reminder that the city doesn't just sleep through history; it shouts, it marches and it makes its voice heard.

Practical Tips
Navigating Paris During a Protest

So, what do you do when Paris throws you into the middle of a protest? Well, you take it in stride, of course! Here are a few tips to help you stay sane and keep your cool during those moments when the city's energy is a little... extra:

- **Check for Updates,** before stepping out, keep an eye on apps like Citymapper or Bonjour RATP for real-time metro and bus info. Protests often cause transport disruptions, so knowing which lines are closed can save you a lot of hassle. There's nothing worse than finding yourself stuck in a packed station with no way to get out—trust me, I've been there.

- **Avoid Protest Hotspots,** demonstrations usually centre around certain iconic spots, like *Place de la République, Place de la Bastille,* or along the *Champs-Élysées.* If you can, steer clear of these areas—not only will you avoid the crowds, but you'll also sidestep any possible chaos. **Pro tip:** checking social media or news websites before heading out can help you pinpoint the areas to avoid.

- **Plan Alternative Routes,** when the usual routes are blocked, think outside the box. Walking, cycling, or hopping on a scooter might be the fastest way to get from A to B.

- **Travel Early or Late,** if you've got somewhere you absolutely must be, aim for off-peak hours. Get up early or wait until after the protest's peak hours—you'll save yourself the stress of fighting your way through crowds. Plus, Paris in the early morning or late evening is beautifully peaceful and gives you a whole different experience of the city.

- **Stay Calm, Stay Safe,** above all, if you find yourself in the thick of things, take a deep breath. Remember that your safety is far more important than making it to your destination on time. Find a safe corner, regroup, and wait for the crowds to clear. In the chaos, it's easy to get flustered, but a calm approach will always get you through.

Potests are as much a part of Paris as the *Seine* that flows through its heart. The vibrant energy that fuels them is woven into the fabric of the city, and learning how to navigate them is just another step in understanding Paris' unique rhythm. So, next time you find yourself swept up in the whirlwind of a demonstration, don't panic! Instead, take a moment to appreciate the spirited, passionate people around you—they're part of what makes Paris Paris. And, hey, at least you'll have a story to tell when you're back at the café with a glass of wine in hand.

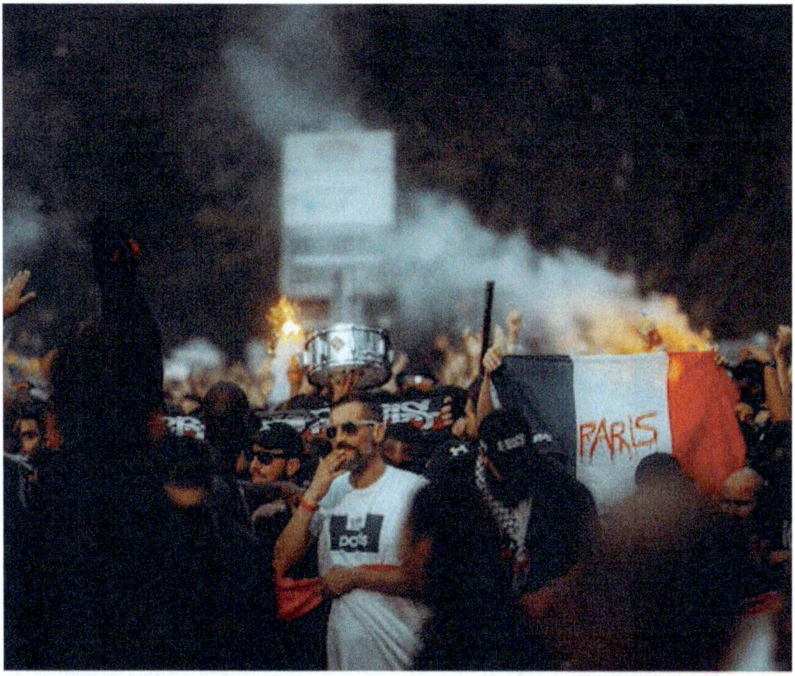
PARIS

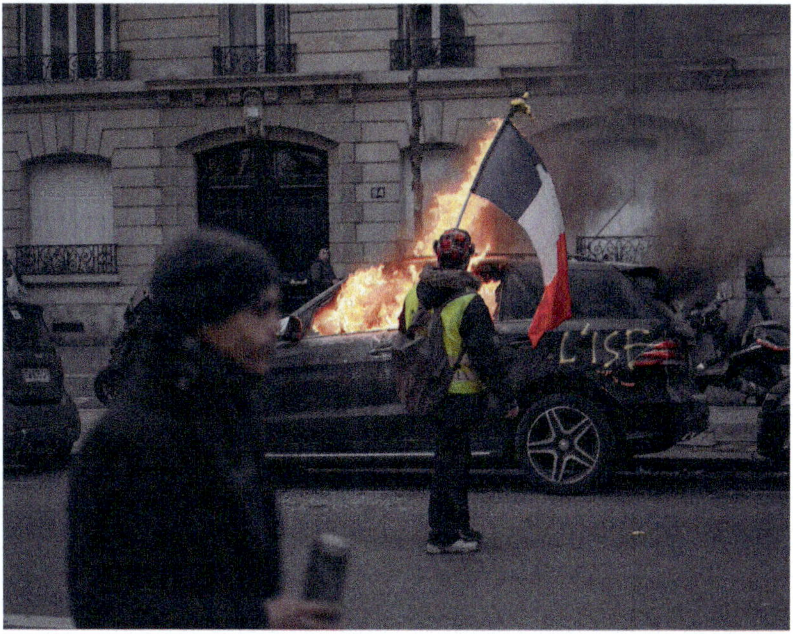

Working in Paris as a Young Expat

There I was, sitting at my laptop, typing *"jobs for English speakers in Paris,"* my stomach a mix of excitement and dread. Moving to a new city is one thing; navigating the job market in a foreign country? That's another story! If you're an expat in Paris, especially if your French skills are limited to *"bonjour," "merci,"* and *"baguette,"* job hunting can feel discouraging, even daunting. The idea of carving out a career in a new place while juggling cultural differences, language barriers, and the constant search for *'le job'* can be enough to make anyone hesitate.

After a month of exploring and settling in, I was ready to dive in headfirst. Armed with a working holiday visa from New Zealand and a whole lot of curiosity, I began scouring the internet for job options. I looked for work that would allow me the flexibility to continue exploring the city and immerse myself in French culture —no easy feat when you're still trying to figure out how to say *"I need directions to the post office"* without sounding like a tourist. Nannying—or working as an au pair—ended up being the perfect choice for me at the time.

I'd never really considered becoming a nanny before, but once I gave it a go, it turned out to be so much more than a job. It was like being handed a front-row ticket to experience French family life in all its chaotic, beautiful glory. I'll never forget sitting at the dinner table with three adorable—energic!—boys, trying to keep up with their rapid-fire French conversation. Some days, I felt like I was learning as much from them as they were from me. For every "*pardon*?" I'd throw out, they'd patiently slow down, only for me to get distracted by the baby brother or the music playing in the background. I don't think I've ever been so culturally immersed—and at times, so exhausted—than in those moments.

It wasn't always easy, but those small moments of cultural exchange made every single challenge worth it. Nannying offered me the opportunity to see Paris through their curious eyes. Through them, I experienced the city in a way that most adults never do. I learned to embrace the quirks of French daily life—the long, leisurely lunches, the endless *bises* (cheek kisses), and the importance of family time.

Looking back, I can't believe how profoundly nannying shaped my experience. It wasn't just about caring for children—it was about understanding the heart of French culture. And it's funny how these things work out, isn't it? The job that seemed like a temporary solution became my gateway into a new world and a new me.

When the time felt right to move on to a new chapter, I shifted gears and began teaching English as a second language at The Turner Learning Centre. It was a whole new ballgame. Gone were the days of playing hide-and-seek in the park or baking delicious cakes in the kitchen. This time, I was in a classroom full of eager French students, each one with their own dreams and challenges.

Those four years of teaching were a journey of discovery. I developed a deeper understanding of the transformative power of language and the connections it creates.

And then came the transition into HR. Looking back, it felt like a natural evolution, like every little lesson I'd learned along the way had come together. From the patience I'd gained with my nannying years to the adaptability I'd cultivated as a teacher, each experience was a stepping stone that led me to this new role.

In HR, I found myself using the communication skills I'd honed and the resilience I'd developed over the years. Paris had shaped me in ways I hadn't fully understood at the time, and as I grew more confident in my career, I realised just how much the city had nurtured my personal development.

The truth is, Paris wasn't just the place where I worked—it was the place that broadened my perspective, and nurtured my personal growth. It taught me to be resilient, flexible, and open to the unexpected twists and turns life throws at you. And the best part? I got to do it all while sipping coffee at quaint cafés, wandering through neighbourhoods I'd never have visited back home, and learning more about myself than I ever could have imagined.

So, whether you're landing in Paris with just a working holiday visa or a dream to discover something new, trust me when I say: the journey may feel intimidating at first, but the rewards are more than worth it. You might not know where you'll end up, but it's the unexpected moments along the way that will leave you feeling more fulfilled than any neatly-planned career path ever could.

And hey, if nothing else, you'll have some cracking stories to tell.

Practical Tips
Job Opportunities You Can Explore

Paris is a city full of opportunities for expats, and the right job can provide a steady income, personal growth and exciting experiences. Whether you're looking to teach, explore your creative talents, or embrace a career in hospitality, Paris has something for everyone. Here are ten job opportunities that you can explore to kickstart your career in the City of Light:

- **English Teacher/Tutor:** Teaching English is one of the most popular jobs for expats, whether in language schools, private institutions, or privately through tutoring students and professionals seeking to enhance their language skills. **Popular employers:** The Turner Learning Centre, Berlitz, Wall Street English.

- **Tour Guide:** If you have a passion for history and culture, working as a tour guide for English-speaking tourists is a rewarding way to share your knowledge of Paris and its landmarks, whether through tour companies or by offering your own specialised tours. **Companies to check out:** Fat Tire Tours, Paris City Vision, Airbnb Experience.

- **Freelance Photographer:** With Paris as a backdrop, freelance photography, whether for weddings, portraits, or travel photography, is a creative way to make a living. **Platforms:** Flytographer, Instagram.

- **Hospitality Management:** With its bustling tourism industry, the city presents abundant opportunities in hotel, restaurant, and bar management. **Major employers:** AccorHotels, Hyatt.

- **Content Creator:** Many expats find work in digital marketing, blogging, copywriting, or content creation. There are often opportunities for English language content creators, especially for companies with international audiences. **Freelance websites:** Upwork, WeWorkRemotely, Remote.co, Fiverr.

- **Digital Nomad (Remote Work):** As a digital nomad, you can live in Paris while working remotely in roles such as web development, graphic design, virtual assistant, or social media management. This flexibility allows you to enjoy Paris without needing to be tied to a French employer. **Platforms:** WeWorkRemotely, Remote.co, Fiverr, Upwork.

- **Chef/Cooking Instructor:** Paris, renowned as the culinary capital of the world, offers an exciting career path for chefs and cooking instructors catering to tourists, expats, and locals. Many expats embark on entrepreneurial journeys by starting small businesses and hosting cooking workshops. **Consider:** Schools like *Le Cordon Bleu,* offer classes through Airbnb Experiences.

- **Translator or Interpreter:** With Paris being a global hub, the need for translation services is high, especially for business and legal purposes. If you are bilingual, working as a translator or interpreter can be a lucrative and flexible job. **Agencies:** Adexen, K International, TransPerfect, Lionbridge, and SDL are known in the industry.

- **Art Gallery/Exhibition Curator:** Paris is an artistic hub, and young expats with a background in Art and/or Design can work as gallery assistants or curators, helping organise exhibitions or manage art collections. **Explore:** Galleries like *Galerie Thaddaeus Ropac* or *Centre Pompidou* for positions.

- **Fitness Instructor/Personal Trainer:** If fitness is your passion, becoming a personal trainer or fitness instructor can be a rewarding career in Paris. There's a growing market for fitness services, especially among the expat community. **Consider:** Joining gyms like Neoness, BasicFit, and Fitness Park or offering private lessons.

Bonus Pro Tips!

Right, now that you've had some to digest all the excitement, let's talk about the practicalities of finding a job in Paris. If you're an expat looking to make your mark, there are plenty of online resources to help you along the way. Here's a little cheat sheet to kick off your job search:

- **LinkedIn** is your ultimate, trusted companion for job hunting and professional connections. It's not just for stalking ex-colleagues (though I'm not judging), it's a serious tool for job seekers and employers alike. Many companies in Paris post job openings here, so you can easily browse listings in your field and connect with professionals who can offer advice or point you in the right direction. It's your gateway to finding out about job opportunities that may not even be advertised elsewhere, and it's perfect for building up your network while you're still figuring out where the best cafés are for working remotely.

- **Indeed France,** one of the most popular job search engines around, Indeed France offers listings across all sorts of sectors. From tech start-ups to traditional industries, you can filter results by salary, job type, and location to narrow down your dream job (or, you know, something that'll pay the rent). What's great is that it also gives you insight into company culture, especially for start-ups, so you can ensure the workplace vibes align with your values. After all, you're in Paris, so let's aim for more *joie de vivre* than stressed-out-office vibes.

- **Glassdoor,** now, here's the real deal: Glassdoor doesn't just give you job listings. It offers company reviews, salary insights, and honest employee feedback. So, if you're wondering what it's really like to work at a certain company in Paris—whether they're great with work-life balance or fantastic at celebrating birthdays—Glassdoor's got you covered. Plus, if you're specifically seeking supportive environments for women (or any underrepresented group), it's an invaluable resource to find workplaces that foster inclusivity and equality.

- **Leboncoin,** if you're looking for something a little more off-beat, Leboncoin might be your new best friend. Think of it like France's version of Craigslist, while it's usually associated with buying second-hand furniture (hello, vintage chic), it's also an excellent place to find local freelance and short-term job opportunities.

Working in Paris can be an incredible adventure, whether you begin as a nanny, an English teacher, or a tour guide. The beauty is that every experience, big or small, will teach you something. Whether it's the art of juggling multiple jobs or learning to navigate French bureaucracy (spoiler: it's an art form), each role will shape your journey in ways you didn't expect.

So, don't stress if your first job isn't your dream job, or if you end up in a role you never thought you'd take. Be open to the unexpected, because Paris is a city that thrives on surprises. And when you start looking back on your time here, you'll realise that the skills and experiences you gather along the way will help you grow in ways you never imagined.

Breaking Down Language Barriers

Let's face it, learning French is terrifying. It's a beautiful language, but those tricky pronunciations and endless verb conjugations can feel like trying to solve a puzzle with constantly shifting pieces. Fear not! With the right strategies, you'll soon be confidently ordering a *croque monsieur* and asking for directions on the metro like a local. The secret? Make French a natural part of your daily life.

When I first arrived in Paris, I had no formal French training. My vocabulary was limited to a few basic words from Duolingo, and I often stumbled through even the simplest phrases. Determined to make progress, I enrolled in a 12-week French course at *Campus Langues* in the 19th *arrondissement*. It was affordable and the perfect starting point for my language journey.

Reflecting on that time, I realised how my role as a nanny became a brilliant bridge between studying and using the language in real-life situations. Through shared meals and playtime with the family, I was immersed in French traditions. I learned how to make *crêpes* and *ratatouille*, practised unfamiliar, and picked up nuances that you'd never find in a textbook.

The structured lessons gave me essential vocabulary and grammar, which made my conversations feel smoother. This mix of classroom learning and real-world application helped break down the language barriers that once seemed so daunting. It transformed learning French from a challenge into a rewarding journey.

Here's the most important thing: you will make mistakes, and that's absolutely fine. The faster you accept this, the quicker you'll progress. No one expects you to get it right immediately, and each slip-up is a learning opportunity. Whether you mix up articles (*le/la*) or ask for a *baguette* instead of a *bague* (ring), it's all part of the process. These moments will turn into funny stories you'll laugh about for years!

The best way to tackle mistakes is with a good sense of humour. If you can laugh at yourself rather than stress over getting it right, you'll stay motivated and keep practising. Every conversation, no matter how bumpy, is another step toward fluency. If someone corrects you, whether it's a friend or the cashier at the bakery, pay attention to their feedback and don't hesitate to repeat it back to lock it into your memory. Asking, "*Est-ce que c'est correct?*" (Is this correct?) can work wonders in accelerating your learning. You'll be surprised at how much you retain just by embracing the process and treating every misstep as part of your linguistic adventure.

So, grab a *croissant aux amandes*, put on your best French accent, and dive in—mistakes and all. Before you know it, you'll be chatting like a true Parisian, not just admiring the language but living it!

Practical Tips
Overcoming Language Barriers

If you're looking to boost your French skills in fun and practical ways, there are plenty of options to explore:

- **Conversation Exchange** is an online platform that connects you with native French speakers for language practice. Whether through virtual video chats or in-person meetups, it offers a relaxed way to improve your fluency.

- **Community centres,** which often run low-cost or free language classes tailored for expats and newcomers. These classes not only help you learn French but also introduce you to the local community and fellow expats. Similarly, check with local town halls (*mairies*), which sometimes offer affordable French classes aimed at helping new residents integrate. While these can be popular and have waiting lists, they provide a supportive environment perfect for beginners.

- **Linguee** is an app that goes beyond basic dictionary functions by showing words and phrases in context. It's fantastic for understanding tricky idiomatic expressions or seeing real-world examples of vocabulary in use.

- For more formal classroom settings, schools like *Alliance Française* and *Campus Langues*, for example, offer a range of courses for all levels, from beginner to advanced. What's more, many of these classes are conversational, meaning you'll start speaking from day one, no need to wait until you've mastered those tricky grammar rules.

- **Podcasts** are another brilliant way to enhance your listening skills. **Coffee Break French** and **FrenchPod101** break down everyday language into bite-sized lessons, perfect for beginners. For those who are a bit more advanced, **InnerFrench** features slow-spoken discussions on fascinating topics, boosting your comprehension. And if you're feeling adventurous, *Les Couilles sur la Table* offers engaging conversations on social issues, filled with colloquial French and real-world slang.

I would also highly recommend starting with the media you already love, such as **films**. Try the whimsical and classic *Le Fabuleux Destin d'Amélie Poulain (Amélie)* or the heartwarming *Intouchables*. For TV, **Extra French**, and **Call My Agent (*Dix pour cent*)** are packed with modern slang and Parisian humour, helping you absorb French in a fun, casual way.

BonusTips!

- Groups like **Blabla Language Exchange Paris** or events on **Meetup.com** bring locals and expats together for casual practice in social settings like cafés or bars. These gatherings are perfect for informal conversations and building friendships while sharpening your language skills.

- Don't forget the small daily habits that can help cement your learning. Change your phone's language settings to French, read menus aloud when dining out, and make it a point to ask questions in French throughout your day.

Learning French may feel overwhelming at first, but each word learned, and every phrase practised brings you closer to fluency and to feeling truly at home in Paris. Embracing mistakes as part of the process, finding joy in small victories, and weaving French into your daily routines will transform language learning from a daunting task into an exciting adventure. Whether you're mastering café orders, navigating new conversations, or laughing at your own language mix-ups, every step forward enriches your experience in the city and connects you more deeply with its culture.

Opening a French Bank Account

Once I settled into my new life in Paris, I quickly realised that opening a local bank account was not just a handy convenience—it was absolutely essential. Between receiving my monthly nanny salary and avoiding the heart-stopping exchange rate fees on my New Zealand card, it became clear that my Parisian adventure required a French bank account. Plus, there's something oddly thrilling about holding a shiny, new bank card with your name on it, ready to swipe!

Armed with optimism and my modest nanny contract, I set out on a mission to open a French bank account. My first stop was a well-known bank, but the consultant barely glanced at my paperwork before explaining with a slight shrug that my income wasn't "*sufficient*" to qualify. Undeterred, I tried another bank. And another.

Each visit left me feeling more like I was auditioning for a role I didn't quite fit—"*Sorry, we're looking for someone with 'more income' for this position.*" It was humbling, to say the least, and a tad frustrating. Was I trying to open a bank account or apply for a mortgage?

Finally, after enough rejections to rival a bad dating streak, I was directed to *Société Générale*. Bracing myself for yet another polite brush-off, I walked in with my documents in hand, anxiety bubbling under the surface. To my surprise, I was greeted by a consultant who spoke decent English and was also—dare I say it—pleasant! She patiently walked me through the steps of opening a basic account, ticked all the necessary boxes, and even managed to smile while doing it. By the end of the appointment, I had my very own French bank account. It felt like winning the expat lottery!

Once the account was set up, it was as if a weight had been lifted. Daily life became infinitely smoother. No more fumbling with cash at the bakery or trying to decipher how many euros my New Zealand dollars would stretch to. Groceries, metro tickets, and even my morning *café au lait* became effortless purchases. And let's not forget the relief of no longer paying absurd foreign transaction fees—my wallet thanked me. Opening that account not only gave me financial stability but also a sense of belonging. I wasn't just visiting Paris anymore; I was truly living here, bank card and all.

Practical Tips
Opening a French Bank Account

Do your research, and consider banks that cater specifically to international clients. Although opening a bank account in France can feel like you're walking through a maze, being aware of these challenges can help you better prepare and choose the right banking partner for your Parisian adventure. Here's a quick rund-own of some reliable French banks and online banking options that make managing your money a breeze.

Traditional French Banks

- *Société Générale:* Known for their English-speaking staff and comprehensive services. You'll need to bring proof of residency, your passport, and a French tax number to get started.

- *BNP Paribas:* One of France's largest banks with a solid reputation and extensive ATM network. They offer services in English, and you can open an account either online or in person.

- *Crédit Agricole:* Particularly friendly to expats, with a dedicated section for international clients. Bring along your ID and proof of residence to set up an account.

Online Banking Apps

- **N26:** A fully digital bank that allows you to manage your finances entirely via smartphone. You can set up an account quickly without requiring French residency, and there are no maintenance fees.

- **Revolut:** Perfect for travellers, offering competitive exchange rates and no foreign transaction fees. Opening an account is instant via their app, and you'll receive a handy debit card.

- **Hello bank!:** A digital service from BNP Paribas designed for tech-savvy users. It combines the convenience of a user-friendly app with the backing of a traditional bank for more complex needs.

Bonus Tips!

- Use comparison websites, platforms like **Selectra** or *MeilleurTaux* can help you compare banking and mobile service plans to find the best deals. Be aware of hidden fees, when choosing a bank, keep an eye on potential fees like maintenance costs or ATM withdrawal charges. Bring the tight documents, always have a copy of your ID, proof of residence, and any other required documents when opening a bank account (or getting a phone plan). It can save you multiple trips.

With my finances in order, I felt empowered to explore the city with confidence and ease. From spontaneous bakery visits to seamless metro rides, these foundational steps made everyday life in Paris more manageable and enjoyable. And while my bank statements occasionally reminded me of my unabashed love for bread, cheese, and wine, they also symbolised my successful integration into the vibrant rhythm of Paris.

Renting Your First Apartment

Finding permanent accommodation in Paris is often one of the biggest challenges for young expats. With its competitive rental market and unique housing customs, securing a long-term place requires preparation, a truckload of patience, and a bit of strategy.

I was full of optimism, picturing myself in a charming flat with a view of the *Eiffel* Tower or beautiful park square. However, reality hit quickly, finding an apartment in this city felt like trying to catch a train that was always just out of reach.

The emotional roller-coaster began almost immediately. I spent hours scrolling through listings, only to discover they were either outrageously expensive, laughably small, or—surprise!—already rented by the time I enquired. I'd send polite emails, attach my meticulously prepared *dossier*, and wait... only to be ghosted. Some listings disappeared so quickly I was convinced landlords had ninja-like reflexes. As the weeks dragged on and Christmas lights began twinkling, my optimism dimmed. I questioned whether I was doomed to an eternal life of temporary accommodation and endless rejection emails.

My dreams of a cosy Parisian apartment felt increasingly like a fantasy, and I braced myself for yet another month of temporary accommodation. But just when I was about to throw in the towel, a new listing popped up! A one-bedroom apartment, located in the 14th *arrondissement*, in a safe neighbourhood that ticked all my boxes. I hesitated for a moment, surely this one would vanish before I had a chance to reach out, right? Well, I decided to take the chance. To my shock, the landlord responded within hours!

Days later, I stood in my new potential home: creaky wooden floors, no lift, a tiny unfurnished kitchen, and the narrowest bathroom I'd ever seen. It wasn't glamorous, and the *Eiffel* Tower was nowhere in sight, but it was mine. After months of searching, I'd found my Parisian flat—and it was perfect (well, perfectly adequate, but that's Paris for you).

Before you sign on the dotted line, let's talk about French housing regulations—because, yes, they do exist, even if they're not always followed. In Paris, the legal minimum size for a rental apartment is nine square metres with a ceiling height of at least 2.20 metres. This is all thanks to the *Loi Carrez*, a French regulation that ensures your flat is liveable.

What does this mean in practice? Your rental must include basic amenities like running water, electricity, heating, and ventilation. If the apartment doesn't meet these standards, it can't legally be rented as a residence. This law is in place to prevent landlords from renting out spaces better suited for storing brooms than housing humans.

So, while Parisian flats are often compact, there are legal limits to how tiny they can be. Keep this in mind as you navigate the rental market—it's one small victory for tenants in a city where finding an apartment feels like winning the lottery.

Practical Tips
Apartment Hunting in Paris

Before you even think about arranging viewings or daydreaming about your perfect Parisian flat, you'll need to prepare a rental *dossier*. Think of this as your tenant CV—a collection of documents that will convince landlords you're the one. Putting it together can feel like a bureaucratic scavenger hunt, requiring proof of income, employment, existence, and, for all they know, your ability to juggle *macarons* while reciting *La Marseillaise*. Make sure to gather the following:

- **ID/Passport:** A copy of your identification.

- **Proof of Income:** Typically, this means three months of pay slips or a work contract. For freelancers and students, you will need a guarantor.

- **Bank Statements:** Three recent months to show financial stability.

- ***RIB (Relevé d'Identité Bancaire):*** Your French bank account details. If you haven't opened an account yet, proof that you're in the process should suffice.

- **Guarantor's Information:** If needed, your guarantor (often French-based) will have to provide their ID, proof of income, and tax returns.

Having these documents ready before you start your search will save you some stress. Trust me, there's nothing worse than spotting your dream apartment, only to realise you're missing a crucial document and watching it slip through your fingers!

Where to Find Rental Listings

Finding long-term rental listings in Paris can be a gruelling task, especially for expats navigating a new city. However, there are several reliable platforms and resources to help you secure a place to call home. Here's a guide to get you started:

Online Platforms

- **Seloger** is a popular real estate website offering a wide range of listings, from furnished apartments to unfurnished flats. The site allows you to filter by neighbourhood, price, and amenities.
- **LeBonCoin,** known for classifieds, this platform also features rental listings. Be cautious of scams, but it's a great resource for direct landlord-to-tenant rentals.
- **Pap.fr,** specialising in direct rentals, PAP eliminates agency fees by connecting you directly with property owners.
- **Green-Acres,** aimed at expats, this site lists properties across France, including long-term rentals in Paris.
- **Paris Attitude** caters specifically to furnished apartments for long-term stays, often ideal for expats and professionals.

Real Estate Agencies

- **Century 21,** is a well-known agency with offices throughout Paris offering long-term rental listings.
- **Foncia** offers a variety of managed properties, providing professional support throughout the rental process.
- **Agence Lodgis** specialises in furnished rentals, often catering to international tenants.

Acting Quickly and Professionally

Once you've found a place that fits your budget and preferences, reach out quickly. Rentals move fast in Paris! Call, email, or message right away to set up a viewing. When you visit the apartment, be prepared:

- **Bring Your *Dossier*,** many landlords will request to see your documents right after the viewing if they're interested.

- **Ask Questions,** inquire about extra charges (building maintenance, utilities etc.) and clarify lease terms, including how long the lease is for and any restrictions.

- **After The Viewing,** submit your complete *dossier*.

In Paris, it's common for landlords to choose the first qualified applicants, so make sure your *dossier* is complete to avoid delays. If you haven't heard back within a couple of days, send a courteous follow-up to express continued interest. If your application is approved:

- **Review the Lease (*Bail*),** the lease should detail the rent, duration, deposit, and any fees.

- **Provide a Security Deposit,** typically, the deposit is one to two months' rent.

- **Set Up Utilities,** check with your landlord or property management for the designated provider. Once you have that information, you can contact the provider to set up your account.

- **Set Up Insurance,** it's mandatory to have home insurance when renting in France. You can obtain this from various companies (**AXA, MAAF, Allianz**), or with your bank.

Bonus Tips!

- **Consider a Guarantor Service:** Don't have a French guarantor? No problem! Services like *Visale*, a free government-backed scheme, can step in and act as your guarantor. It's a lifesaver for expats.

- **Start Early:** Begin your search the moment you have a job offer in hand—especially if it's a *Contrat à Durée Indéterminée (CDI)*, which is a permanent contract. Having a CDI can make you a much more appealing candidate to landlords.

- **Think About the Location:** Prioritise neighbourhoods with good public transport links, especially near metro lines. Avoid areas too far from the city centre unless you're prepared for longer commutes. Trust me, you'll want that extra snooze time in the mornings!

- **Be Flexible:** The perfect apartment might not exist (or might be snapped up in seconds), so focus on what matters—safe neighbourhoods, comfortable living conditions, and something within your budget. Your dream *Eiffel* Tower view can come later.

Apartment hunting in Paris takes patience and persistence, but with a prepared *dossier* and the right mindset, you will find your place. Keep a positive outlook, and before you know it, you'll be settling into your new Parisian life—*baguette* in hand and a sense of triumph in your heart!

Embracing the Café Lifestyle

The café culture in Paris is world-famous for a reason. These aren't just places to grab a quick coffee—they're social hubs, extensions of living rooms, and sometimes, even makeshift offices. From dawn till dusk, Parisians flock to cafés to sip, chat, read, or simply let time pass as they soak up the city's charm. Embracing this lifestyle is one of the quickest ways to feel like a true Parisian (beret optional, but highly recommended).

Forget Netflix—Parisian cafés offer the best free entertainment in town. Outdoor seating is often arranged theatre-style, with all chairs facing the street. Why? Because the streets of Paris are the ultimate stage, and the actors are everyone from chic locals rushing to work, artists sketching quietly in the corner, to starry-eyed tourists snapping photos of every French pastry in sight.

With a *boisson* (drink) in hand and a front-row seat, you're set for hours of people-watching. There's something mesmerising about observing life in motion—the dramas, the romances, the eccen-tricities. And don't worry about looking too curious; in Paris, being nosy is practically an art form.

Practical Tips
How to Café Like a Parisian

Forget the grab-and-go culture you might be used to. In Paris, the café ritual is all about taking your time. Here, you're not just drinking a beverage; you're engaging in a sacred act of leisure. It's entirely normal—expected, even—to linger over your espresso for hours, whether you're engrossed in a book, having a deep conversation, or simply daydreaming. Ordering is delightfully straightforward:

- Ask for a *café* and you'll get a strong, no-frills *espresso*.

- Want something milkier? Try a *café crème* or *café au lait*.

- Feeling fancy? Opt for a *café noisette*, an espresso with a splash of milk.

And when it's time to pay, don't wave your card around the moment your drink lands on the table. Parisians settle up when they're ready to leave, often with a casual, *"L'addition, s'il vous plaît."*

A Parisian café isn't just a place—it's a lifestyle. It's about savouring moment of break, embracing the rhythm of the city, and learning that life doesn't always have to be rushed. Whether you're sipping your morning coffee or watching the sunset with a glass of wine, a café table is where you'll find your groove in Paris.

So, take a seat, order something delicious, and let the city's magic unfold before you. Cheers to living like a local—one sip at a time!

Balancing Work and Leisure

When I first landed in Paris, I threw myself into a frenzy of errands, thinking I could breeze through the day ticking off my to-do list. And then it happened. I approached the bank one afternoon, brimming with optimism, only to be greeted by a sign that said: "*Fermé de 12h à 14h.*" Closed for two hours in the middle of the day? I stood there, bewildered, while Parisians around me strolled leisurely to their *déjeuner* (lunch), completely unfazed.

You see, the French lunch break isn't just a quick sandwich on the go. It's an event. Offices, shops, and yes, even banks, shut their doors, and people actually sit down to enjoy their meals. This tradition is deeply rooted in French culture, which places a strong emphasis on enjoying meals and taking proper breaks throughout the day. It's more than just a quick lunch, it's an opportunity to pause and relish the moment. These breaks weren't merely about stepping away from work, they were about connecting with people and enjoying life's simple pleasures.

Let's talk about the magic of *Apéro*. After a day's work, Parisians don't just go home—they make time to enjoy life. Enter *l'apéro*,

the magical window between work and dinner, where the only is to unwind. Friends gather for pre-dinner drinks at a café or bar, nibbling on olives or crisps, chatting, and letting the stresses of the day dissolve. It didn't take me long to adopt this tradition wholeheartedly. After a particularly long week at school, I'd join friends for a glass of wine or a beer, and we'd talk about anything and everything. These moments of relaxation became my lifeline—a slice of joy that made me feel like I'd unlocked a secret chapter of Parisian life.

Now, Sundays in Paris. Don't expect a shopping spree or a whirlwind of errands. Most businesses shut, except for some restaurants and grocery stores, leaving the city blissfully calm. Instead, Sundays are for long walks along the *Seine*, picnics in parks, or leisurely meals with friends. Watching Parisians effortlessly switch gears from being highly efficient during the week to fully disconnecting over the weekend was a revelation. They were privy to a secret I had yet to learn, how to truly savour moments of relaxation.

And then there's August. One day, the city feels alive with its usual buzz, and the next, it's eerily quiet. Why? Because Parisians take vacation seriously. Many flee to the coast or countryside, leaving the city to the tourists. At first, I was baffled by the sudden emptiness. But soon, I realised the beauty of it. Without the usual crowds, I explored hidden gems, lingered in quiet cafés, and enjoyed a slower, more intimate version of Paris. This rhythm, this *"profiter de la vie"* (to enjoy life), became something I cherished.

Living in Paris taught me a lesson I didn't know I needed: it's okay to slow down. It's okay to take time for yourself, to savour a moment, and to prioritise joy. From long lunches to quiet Sundays, from *apéro* evenings to extended summer breaks, Parisians understand that life is about balance.

And slowly, I started to understand it too. So, if you're new to Paris, take a deep breath. Lean into the slower moments. Relish the laughter with friends, the stillness of a Sunday, or the sweetness of an hour spent sipping wine at a café. Because in Paris, life is meant to be savoured, not rushed.

Adopting the Picnic Culture

If there's one thing Parisians do with unmatched flair, it's picnics. The moment the city shakes off its winter coat and the first hint of sunshine appears, parks and riversides transform into buzz-ing open-air dining rooms. From the lush lawns of the *Jardin des Tuileries* to the hills of *Parc des Buttes-Chaumont,* you'll find every patch of grass claimed by blankets, baskets, and *baguettes*. Families, friends, and couples gather, turning these public spaces into a sea of artisanal cheeses, crusty bread, *saucisson*, fresh fruit, and—of course—bottles of wine.

Naturally, I was eager to join the fun. Inspired by this delightful culture, I grabbed what I assumed were the essentials: a *baguette*, a wedge of cheese, and a bottle of wine. Feeling very Parisian (or so I thought), I made my way to the banks of the *Seine* to meet some classmates from my French course. We found a spot with a perfect view of *Notre-Dame*, ready to embrace the ultimate Parisian pastime.

As we spread out on the embankment, I beamed with pride. I'd nailed this picnic preparation thing!

That is, until I unpacked my bag. Bread? Check. Cheese? Check. Wine? Check. Corkscrew? Oh no.

I rummaged through my bag, hoping I'd magically stashed one without realising. But no. The bottle of wine sat smugly in front of me, its cork a mocking reminder of my rookie mistake. Around us, seasoned Parisians poured wine with ease, laughing and chatting as if they'd been born with corkscrews in hand.

Just as I began contemplating the physics of opening a bottle with a pen (spoiler: it doesn't work...), a nearby couple caught my eye. With a knowing smile, they leaned over and offered their corkscrew, saying with a playful laugh, *"C'est indispensable pour un pique-nique !"* (It's indispensable for a picnic!). Lesson learned. Never, ever attempt a picnic without one.

With our wine finally flowing, I settled back to take in the scene. The *Seine* glimmered in the afternoon light, the breeze carried the faint aroma of fresh bread, and laughter rippled through the air. I noticed how unhurried everyone seemed, savouring each bite of cheese and every sip of wine as if they had all the time in the world.

Parisians treat picnics not as a rushed meal but as an event. It's about the company, the conversation, and the simple joy of being outdoors. People shared stories, debated the best *boulangeries* in town, and occasionally waved at passing boats. Children played nearby, couples strolled hand in hand, and even the pigeons seemed to enjoy the vibe.

That day by the *Seine* became one of my favourite Parisian memories—not because of the cheese or the wine (although they were excellent), but because of the laughter, the kindness of strangers, and the reminder to enjoy life's simple pleasures.

Practical Tips
How to Picnic Like the Parisians

That first picnic taught me a few valuable lessons, and soon I had developed my own Parisian Picnic Formula. Here's how you can embrace the art of the Parisian picnic:

- **Pack the Essentials:** Head to your nearest bakery for a fresh baguette, grab some cheese from a local *fromagerie*, and don't forget a bottle of wine or sparkling water. Parisians love to keep it simple but delicious!

- **Wine Opener:** If you're bringing along a bottle of French wine (which is highly recommended), don't forget a corkscrew! This is an item most Parisians will always carry with them during the summer, and after my first picnic, I never left home without one in my bag.

- **Reusable Utensils and Plates:** Skip the plastic and opt for eco-friendly reusable utensils, plates, and cups. It's better for the environment and adds a touch of Parisian sophistication to your picnic.

- **Choosing Your Spot:** One of the joys of picnicking in Paris is the sheer variety of beautiful locations to choose from. Whether you prefer the riverbanks or the expansive city parks, there's no shortage of picturesque spots to lay down your blanket. Some of the best picnic spots in the city are along the *Seine*, especially near *Ile de la Cité* or *Ile Saint-Louis*, or in parks like *Jardin des Tuileries, Parc des Buttes-Chaumont*, or the iconic *Champ-de-Mars*, with the *Eiffel* Tower as your backdrop.

- **Gather Some Friends:** Picnics are often a social affair. Invite friends or colleagues, or head out solo and embrace the communal atmosphere. Even if you're alone, you're never alone. The atmosphere is contagious, people share smiles and lend each other corkscrews, and there's always a hum of laughter and conversation in the air.

- **Bring a Blanket:** A small, portable blanket or even a cloth will do. Parisians love spreading out in style, with some even bringing portable picnic baskets and wine glasses to enhance the experience. I always make sure to carry a scarf (specifically for this purpose!) where I go now, and it's amazing how quickly you feel part of the culture when you lay out your little spot of comfort.

- **Time It Right:** While you can picnic at any time, evenings in the summer are magical. People linger after sunset, and the city lights add a special touch to the experience. There's something almost dreamlike about watching the sun dip behind the city, the soft glow of the evening settling in as the *Eiffel* Tower twinkles in the distance. It's the kind of beauty that takes your breath away and makes you fall in love with Paris all over again.

So, the next time the sun is shining, and you have a free afternoon, grab a bottle of wine, gather some friends, or solo, and head to one of Paris' stunning picnic spots. After a while, you stop checking the clock and start measuring the evening by the number of laughs shared, the last drop of wine, or the softening light of the day's end. You might just find that, like me, you'll never want to leave!

Integrating into French Traditions

Paris isn't just famous for its art, fashion, and rich history—it's a city that comes alive with vibrant cultural events and lively festivals throughout the year. These celebrations are not only a reflection of the city's artistic and historical heritage but also a testament to the French way of life. From national holidays that stir patriotism to local traditions that highlight the community's spirit, each event offers a unique opportunity to experience Paris in a deeper, more meaningful way.

Paris's festivals bring together Parisians and visitors alike, offering a sense of unity and joy, while showcasing the diversity of the city's cultural landscape. With a calendar full of events, from intimate neighbourhood gatherings to grand public celebrations, there's always something to discover. Paris's dynamic festival scene invites you to dive right into the action, creating unforgettable experiences and lasting memories. So, whether you're a first-time visitor or a seasoned traveller, mark your calendar and prepare to immerse yourself in the true spirit of Parisian life, where every season brings a new reason to celebrate!

La Fête Nationale (Bastille Day)

Held every 14th of July, *Bastille* Day is France's biggest national holiday—and Paris pulls out all the stops. The day kicks off with a grand military parade down the *Champs-Élysées*, a dazzling fireworks display over the *Eiffel* Tower, and street parties that stretch late into the night. The real secret to celebrating like a local? Attend the *Bals des Pompiers*, lively parties hosted by fire stations across the city on the night before. Picture this: mingling with Parisian firefighters, sipping cold beers, and dancing the night away to live music and DJs. Each fire station adds its own flair to the festivities, creating an electrifying, unforgettable atmosphere.

Fête de la Musique

Every 21st of June, Paris transforms into a massive open-air music festival for *Fête de la Musique*. This annual event, which began in 1982, has grown into one of the city's most beloved celebrations, filling every corner of Paris with music from dusk till dawn. Whe-ther you're in a lively neighbourhood square, a quiet street, or a grand public park, you'll find musicians of all types—from professional orchestras to street performers—turning Paris into one giant concert hall. On this day, the entire city becomes a stage for music lovers of all kinds. From classical orchestras playing in the grand spaces of the *Place de la Concorde*, to rock bands jamming on street corners, and jazz musicians filling the air with improvisation, there's a style for every taste. It's a unique way to experience the spirit of Paris, as the music echoes through the streets, creating an atmosphere of spontaneous celebration.

Nuit Blanche (White Night)

Every October, *Nuit Blanche* turns Paris into a citywide art exhibition. Museums, galleries, and even metro stations transform into stages for stunning art installations, performances, and creative surprises. It's an adventure of discovery, as even unexpected spots like bridges and parks become immersive art experiences. Whether you're an art aficionado or just curious, this magical night is a chance to see Paris in a whole new light—literally.

Paris Plages (Paris Beaches)

From July to August, the *Seine* and *Bassin de la Villette* transform into urban beach escapes complete with sand, sun loungers, and parasols. Whether you're kayaking, playing *pétanque*, or sipping a cool drink under the shade of a parasol, *Paris Plages* brings a slice of the seaside to the heart of the city. Perfect for families, friends, or solo visitors, this free summer tradition combines relaxation with fun activities, music, and food stands.

Paris Jazz Festival (Summer)

Set in the lush *Parc Floral*, the Paris Jazz Festival offers a series of open-air concerts every summer weekend. Surrounded by greenery and the soothing melodies of live jazz, it's the perfect way to spend a sunny afternoon, whether you're a die-hard jazz fan or simply in the mood for good music in a stunning setting.

Beaujolais Nouveau

Every November, the third Thursday marks the arrival of *Beaujolais Nouveau* wine. Head to a local wine bar to join the celebrations, complete with tastings, lively conversation, and themed decor. It's a fantastic way to mingle with locals while sipping on the year's fruity new vintage, often paired with music and special snacks.

Marché de Noël (Christmas Markets)

As the festive season approaches, Paris sparkles with Christmas markets from late November to December. Stroll through markets like those at the *Champs-Élysées* or *Montmartre*, where you'll find handcrafted gifts, seasonal treats, and mulled wine. The atmosphere is pure magic—perfect for soaking up the holiday spirit.

Bonus Tips for Major Events!

- For *Bastille* Day, arrive early for a prime spot to watch the fireworks. Be prepared for busy public transport—it's worth the wait!
- For *Nuit Blanche*, plan a few key stops in advance but leave room for spontaneous discoveries.
- For *Paris Plages*, pack sunscreen and embrace the laid-back vibes—don't miss an evening stroll along the *Seine*.

Paris's festivals aren't just events—they're an invitation to join in the city's *joie de vivre*—the joy of living, connect with its people, and create unforgettable memories. Whatever the season, there's always something to celebrate in the City of Light!

Making Connections in
the Heart of Paris

When I first arrived in Paris, homesickness started creeping in like a shadow. Culture shock was like an uninvited guest who made themselves far too comfortable in my head. But then, during one of my many late-night internet sessions, I stumbled upon the Netball Paris Club while mindlessly browsing. Having played netball back in New Zealand, I thought, *"Why not give it a shot?"* From the moment I stepped onto the court, I was hit by an overwhelming sense of familiarity, as though the court had somehow turned into my second home. And just like that, I found myself surrounded by new friends, both French and English-speaking. Weekly netball sessions soon became the highlight of my week.

Not only did the sport keep me fit, but it also gave me a much-needed break from the usual Parisian grind. The thrill of the game, mixed with the joy of chatting with friends, created a perfect balance in my life. Every practice was filled with laughter and camaraderie, and I couldn't help but look forward to those sessions more than I'd anticipated. Whether we were sweating it out during warm-ups or engaging in friendly competition, each

session reminded me of the simple joys that sports bring. And, of course, no practice was ever complete without heading to a nearby *bistro* afterwards for a drink or coffee with the team.

These post-game hangouts quickly became a cherished part of my routine. Whether we were celebrating victories or just chatting about life, I began to feel like I was carving out my own space in Paris. What started as a simple sporting hobby turned into my life-line—grounding me in the city and helping me embrace the Parisian lifestyle, while building lasting friendships.

Practical Tips
Getting Out and Making Friends

Join Social Groups or Classes

Take trial classes, many studios and organisations offer trial classes at a reduced rate or even for free. Try a few to see where you feel most comfortable before committing to one. Set a weekly goal, and challenge yourself to join at least one social activity each week, whether it's a class, workshop, or event. This keeps your schedule balanced between socialising and other commitments. Engage before and after class, don't rush in and out of class, arrive a few minutes early and stay a little afterwards to chat with others. These informal moments are ideal for making connections.

Engage Before and After Class

Don't rush in and out of class, arrive a few minutes early and stay a little afterwards to chat with others. These informal moments are ideal for making connections. Leverage language exchange events, prepare conversation starters, and think of a few topics or questions in both English and French (or any other language you're learning) that you can use to break the ice at these events. Follow-up afterwards, if you've clicked with someone, suggest meeting up again outside the event, whether for a coffee or to attend another language exchange together. Make it a routine, attending the same event consistently helps build familiarity.

Be a Regular at Your Local Spots

Learn the basics in French, and master basic greetings and small talk to engage with locals. Even simple phrases like *"Bonjour, comment ça va?"* can make a difference. Go at the same time each day, and create a routine by visiting your local café or market at the same time. Familiar faces will start to recognise you, leading to more chances for interaction. Compliment, ask questions, compliment the barista on your coffee or ask for recommendations at the market. Engaging with small comments can open the door to more extended conversations.

Join Sports Teams and Leagues

Join open practices, many sports leagues host open practices or friendly games where anyone is welcome to join, regardless of skill level. It's a relaxed way to get active, meet new people, and immerse yourself in the local expat or Parisian scene. Plus, it's a great way to feel part of something, even if you're still getting to grips with the city. Volunteering and getting involved, helping with team logistics, managing equipment, or organising social outings is a brilliant way to connect with others and make yourself known. Not only does it give you the chance to contribute, but it also creates stronger bonds with teammates, often, the best friendships begin while you're folding up kits or handing out drinks!

Plan casual meetups, after a match or practice, why not suggest grabbing a drink or a bite to eat? It's a perfect opportunity to chat and get to know your teammates outside of the game. These relaxed gatherings are often where real connections are made, especially when you're in a new city and craving that sense of community.

Bonus Tip!

- Say **"yes!"** as often as possible to social invites, especially in your first few months of settling in Paris. You never know what amaz-ing surprises await you!

Finding common ground is essential when building friendships, and in Paris, there are countless opportunities to connect through shared interests and hobbies. Whether you're enthusiastic about art, sports, music, or wine, there's a community of people who share that interest. By engaging in activities that you genuinely enjoy, you'll naturally meet others who align with your passions, making it easier to bond and create meaningful relationships.

Exploring Life Beyond the City

Taking day trips out of Paris can be a refreshing escape. It's also a chance to experience the charm of the French countryside and nearby towns. While the city itself is packed with wonders, there's an entire world of beauty just a short train ride away. From the lush gardens of *Giverny* to the *Palace of Versailles*, or even the fairytale streets of medieval towns like *Provins*, each destination offers a unique glimpse into France's rich history and culture, that you won't want to miss!

The best part? It's incredibly easy and affordable to arrange! The French train system (SNCF) makes it a breeze to hop on a train from central Paris. Many tickets for regional destinations are very reasonably priced, often starting at around €10–€20, especially if you book in advance or travel off-peak. Plus, with trains running frequently, you needn't worry about complicated schedules. You can decide on a whim to explore beyond the city and be back by evening, making it the perfect option for spontaneous travellers or anyone looking to add an extra layer of excitement to their Parisian experience. So, pack your picnic, grab your train ticket, and let's go!

Bonus Tips!
Great Destinations to Visit Outside of Paris

Versailles

Just 30 minutes by train, *Versailles* is a dazzling retreat into France's royal past. The *Château de Versailles*, with its breathtaking Hall of Mirrors, extravagant royal apartments, and lavishly decorated rooms, show-cases the height of opulence. Outside, the meticulously landscaped gardens stretch for miles, featuring fountains, statues, and charming hidden groves. Take your time exploring this grand palace and its grounds and embrace the royal atmosphere in true *Versailles* style!

Giverny

Just over an hour from Paris by train, the enchanting village of *Giverny* is a must-visit destination, celebrated as the home of the renowned Impressionist painter Claude Monet. Nestled in the heart of *Normandy, Giverny* offers a serene escape from the bustling city, inviting visitors to step into the tranquil world that inspired some of the most iconic works in art history. Monet's house, carefully preserved and colourfully adorned, provides a fascinating glimpse into the artist's life and his love of nature. The highlight, however, is undoubtedly the magnificent gardens, a painter's dream and a haven for photographers and nature lovers alike.

Lille

Only about an hour from Paris by high-speed train, *Lille* is a vibrant northern city that combines French and Flemish influences in an utterly charming way. Known for its distinctive architecture, cobbled streets, and bustling squares, *Lille* has a personality all its own. The city's *Grand Place* is a stunning showcase of 17th-century Flemish architecture, while the *Vieille Bourse*, a former stock exchange with its ornate facade and inner courtyard, exudes historical charm and is a perfect spot to browse for old books and trinkets. With its friendly atmosphere, historic beauty, and distinctive culinary offerings, *Lille* is a delightful day trip for anyone looking to experience a different side of France.

Reims

A quick 45-minute journey from Paris by high-speed train brings you to *Reims*, the celebrated heart of France's *Champagne* region. Known worldwide for its sparkling wines, *Reims* offers visitors a chance to tour some of the world's most prestigious champagne houses, such as *Veuve Clicquot, Taittinger,* and *Pommery*. Stroll around *Place Drouet d'Erlon*, the city's lively main square filled with cafés, boutiques, and restaurants serving local delicacies. By the end of the day, you'll feel fully immersed in the charm, history, and elegance that make *Reims* such a beloved day trip. Just don't overdo the bubbly before catching your train back!

Dijon

Just an hour and a half by high-speed train, *Dijon* is a must-visit for food and history lovers. Known for its famous mustard and Burgundy wines, this historic town features a beautiful **UNESCO**-listed centre with medieval and *Renaissance* architecture. Wander through *Les Halles* Market, designed by *Gustave Eiffel*, to sample local cheeses, spiced bread, and *Dijon's* speciality mustards. Don't miss the Palace of the Dukes and the striking *Notre-Dame* Church. Wrap up with a wine tasting to savour Burgundy's finest, *Dijon* is a true treat for the senses!

Fontainebleau

Only 40 minutes by train, *Fontainebleau* is perfect for a day trip steeped in nature and history. The town is renowned for its expansive forest, a favourite spot for hikers and rock climbers alike. At its heart lies the magnificent *Château de Fontainebleau*, a grand *Renaissance* palace that hosted French royalty for centuries, including Napoleon. Wander through lavishly decorated halls, royal apartments, and lush gardens, it's a truly regal escape just outside of Paris!

Provins

Step back in time with a visit to *Provins*, a **UNESCO World Heritage** medieval town just over an hour from Paris by train. Wander through its cobbled streets, explore ancient ramparts, and marvel at the *Tour César*, a striking 12th-century watchtower. Don't miss the underground tunnels and the *Saint-Quiriace Collegiate* Church for a glimpse into its fascinating past. Known for its medieval festivals and rose-based delicacies, *Provins* offers an enchanting day trip steeped in history and charm.

Epilogue

As we reach the end of this journey, I hope you feel inspired to embrace your own adventure in this remarkable city. Paris is more than just the iconic landmarks or delicious cuisine. It's about immersing yourself in a vibrant culture, forming connections, and creating a life that resonates with your passions.

Throughout this guide, we've explored essential aspects of Parisian life, from discovering the culture and participating in local traditions to forging lasting friendships. Each chapter highlights the joys and challenges of being an expat, emphasising the importance of openness, patience, and a sense of adventure.

Remember, Paris rewards those who take the time to savour its moments. It invites you to pause and appreciate the beauty around you, whether in a quiet park, a bustling market, or during lively gatherings with friends. As you step into your own Parisian experience, let curiosity be your guide.

Embrace the unexpected, be open to new friendships, and don't shy away from missteps, each experience adds to the rich tapestry of your life in this enchanting city.

And know that you are not alone, countless others have walked these cobbled streets and discovered the magic within. Armed with the tools and insights from this guide, I have no doubt you will create beautiful memories in this dreamy city.

Thank you for joining me on this journey. May your time in Paris be filled with laughter, learning, and love, and may you always find joy in the little moments that make life extraordinary.

Bon voyage, and welcome to your new home!

"Il n'est rien d'impossible à celui qui veut."

— Alexandre le Grand

"Nothing is impossible for the one who wills."
This timeless saying encourages determination and belief in one's
ability to overcome challenges and achieve greatness.

Printed in Great Britain
by Amazon

52913270R00076